BOOKS

One Small Suitcase

Barry Turner has a PhD in Political History and has been a full-time writer for thirty years. He has worked as a journalist and broadcaster in various fields, including politics, biography, travel and education, and is the author of over twenty books, including the bestselling *A Place in the Country*, which became a television series, and ... *And the Policeman Smiled*, the story of ten thousand refugee children who escaped to Britain just before the war. He is a regular contributor to *The Times* as a book reviewer, and is editor of the annual *Writer's Handbook*.

D1149800

Barry Turner

One Small Suitcase

PUFFIN BOOKS

PUFFIN BOOKS

Published by the Penguin Group
Penguin Books Ltd, 80 Strand, London WC2R 0RL, England
Penguin Putnam Inc., 375 Hudson Street, New York, New York 10014, USA
Penguin Books Australia Ltd, 250 Camberwell Road, Camberwell, Victoria 3124, Australia
Penguin Books Canada Ltd, 10 Alcorn Avenue, Toronto, Ontario, Canada M4V 3B2
Penguin Books India (P) Ltd, 11 Community Centre, Panchsheel Park, New Delhi – 110 017, India
Penguin Books (NZ) Ltd, Cnr Rosedale and Airborne Roads, Albany, Auckland, New Zealand
Penguin Books (South Africa) (Pty) Ltd, 24 Sturdee Avenue, Rosebank 2196, South Africa

Penguin Books Ltd, Registered Offices: 80 Strand, London WC2R 0RL, England

www.penguin.com

First published 2003
1

Copyright © Barry Turner, 2003
'All the Leaves Have Lost Their Trees' by Gerda Mayer, first published in
The Knockabout Show, Chatto Poets for the Young, Chatto & Windus, 1978
All rights reserved

The moral right of the author has been asserted

Set in Linotype Joanna
Typeset by Rowland Phototypesetting Ltd, Bury St Edmunds, Suffolk

Made and printed in England by Clays Ltd, St Ives plc

Except in the United States of America, this book is sold subject to
the condition that it shall not, by way of trade or otherwise, be lent, re-sold, hired out,
or otherwise circulated without the publisher's prior consent in any form of binding or
cover other than that in which it is published and without a similar condition
including this condition being imposed on the subsequent purchaser

British Library Cataloguing in Publication Data
A CIP catalogue record for this book is available from the British Library

ISBN 0–141–31469–9

COVENTRY SCHOOLS LIBRARY SERVICE	
20-Mar-03	J940.53
PETERS	

ALL THE LEAVES HAVE LOST THEIR TREES
(For Hannah who said it)

All the leaves have lost their trees.
Child, what tumbled words are these?
(Yet I grieve for my lost tree:
Far away the wind bore me.)

Gerda Mayer

Contents

Contents

Introduction

. . . and the Policeman Smiled

Imagine this. It is an autumn evening and there is a chill wind blowing as you make your way home. The light over the front door is welcoming. As you let yourself in, shaking off the cold, you hear your parents laughing and joking. The smell of cooking tells you that a good meal is soon to be enjoyed. You make your way to the dining room where the family is gathered round the table. Everybody is talking at once so, at first, a noise outside, shouting and people running in the street, goes unnoticed. But then there is a loud knock at the door. Who can that be? It is your mother who goes to find out. There is a scream and the next thing you know, young men in grey and black shirts are pushing their way into the room. Your father gets up to demand to know what is happening, but he is knocked to the ground. The table is tipped up, chairs thrown against the wall, ornaments smashed. When at last the men go away, there is a long, long silence. It all happened in a few minutes, but the horrible scene will stay with you for the rest of your life.

Incredible? Yet there are people living today who remember it happening to them. And not in some far off place that civilization had barely touched, but at the heart of Europe in what is today one of the world's leading democracies.

Seventy years ago, Germany was in chaos. Defeated in the First World War of 1914–18, the once-proud country slid from one crisis to another as its citizens tried to come to terms with the death and destruction that had wrecked their economy and made them the outcasts of Europe. Against this background, political extremists, with their talk of leadership, discipline and obedience, began to make an impact. People were drawn to politicians who promised a quick cure for Germany's problems by getting rid of the old government. One political party in particular, the National Socialists or Nazis, attracted so much support that by 1933 they were strong enough to form a new government. Their leader was Adolf Hitler.

Hitler and his supporters were not the type to tolerate any form of opposition to their party and, as they tightened their grip on the country, they made sure that whenever there were problems or setbacks, it was always someone else's fault. A favourite theme was to put the blame on people who were said to be unpatriotic Germans helping to destroy the country for their own selfish ends. The chief target of the bitter and increasingly aggressive propaganda was the Jews.

Anti-Jewish feeling, more commonly known as anti-Semitism, has a long history, starting with the age-old arguments about who was responsible for Christ's crucifixion. But in more modern times, the Jews often suffered persecution simply because they were different: a minority with their own traditions, customs and religious beliefs. When times were hard it was easy to take out frustration and anger on those who set themselves apart from ordinary society. This is what happened in Germany in the 1930s. The Nazi campaign against the Jews was cruel and dishonest, and it led to one of the most shameful chapters in twentieth-century history: the herding of Jewish families into concentration camps where millions were killed or starved to death.

But to go back to the beginning: when Hitler came to power in January 1933, few imagined the extent of the horrors in store. Many took the optimistic view that the Nazis talked such nonsense the public would soon turn against them. Even after a nationwide boycott of Jewish shops and businesses and numerous acts of unprovoked violence, a mood of hope prevailed in many German Jewish communities. Listening to his parents and friends, young Philip Urbach – not then dreaming that in less than four years he would be leaving his home near Leipzig forever – shared the conviction that 'the old shame of defeat in the First World War had been erased and that a bright future was beckoning the Germans'.

The popular feeling of security among German

Jews was rooted in a strong sense of national identity. After all, they had been part of German history for a thousand years. German industry, law, medicine, science, literature and art drew heavily on Jewish talent. Surely, it was argued, the Nazis would not sacrifice so much achievement?

It was soon to be proved otherwise.

Chapter One

The Nazis Take Control

The first victims of Nazi persecution were the children. As early as April 1933, not long after Hitler came to power, German state schools were told to cut the number of Jewish students to under five per cent of their intake. But it was those Jewish children who did go to school who often suffered more than those who were forced to stay away.

Johnny Eichwald, aged twelve, was at a school in north Germany, just twenty-eight miles from the border with Denmark. His father was a tobacconist, the only Jewish trader in the small town of Kappelin.

Teachers started calling me 'Jewboy' in front of the class. And even my friends in the class got so used to it, they didn't even know what it meant. Every year there was a sports day and we used to have shooting. Now, in this particular year I was the best shot. I had three shots right into the bullseye, but when the prizes were given out I was put in second place. I heard one of my school-friends tell a teacher: 'There must have been a mistake, surely Johnny had three?' And the reply was: 'We can't have a Jewboy as king of the shots.' I was very upset about it.

Even the youngest children had a hard time. Edith Birkenruth was born in Neustadt, near Bremen. Her family, of Dutch descent, had lived there for more than a hundred years.

At the age of six I had to go to the regular school, and the first thing that greeted me was the children saying that I was a dirty Jew and I must eat in the toilet. My brother and I were the only Jewish children in the school and we had to eat our sandwiches in the toilet – the teachers were aware of this but did nothing. Classes were all right at first, but then, here and there would be a very anti-Semitic teacher who would do things such as send me out of the classroom saying I was a Jew and I didn't have to learn this and then call me back in and ask me questions. She would then say to the others: 'You see, the Jews aren't all that clever; they don't know everything.' She liked to make fun of me and my brother. The children would laugh; they thought it was very funny.

There were teachers who were more understanding, as Hannele Zürndorfer remembers:

At school the class no longer stood up and chorused: 'Good morning, Fräulein Ratchen!' when the teacher came in; instead we had to stand up, thrust out our arms and shout, '*Heil Hitler!*' I never quite knew whether to join in or not. I knew Hitler was evil and the cause of all our troubles, but felt afraid not to raise my hand. Fräulein Ratchen told me quietly one day that I need not do it.

Meanwhile, there were yet more restrictions on how Jewish families could live their lives. In 1935, Jews lost their right to German citizenship. This meant that they could no longer get jobs as civil servants or practise in one of the professions, such as law or medicine, or even vote in elections. A year on, discrimination against Jewish children was made official; they could no longer mix with other children. Peter Praeger was at school in Berlin:

Things were getting difficult for Jewish boys. Some teachers were outright anti-Semitic. Our PE teacher, Herr Neumann, would make the entire class do punishment PE drills 'because one of the Jewboys didn't pay attention'.

We had special lessons, called National Politics. One topic was called Racial Theory. According to our teacher, who was a professor of biology, the world was divided into a number of races, which could be distinguished by the shape of their skulls. The highest development occurred in the Germanic Longheads. In order to prove his point, the professor made us three Jewish children stand up. He asked me to come to the front of the class. The teacher explained that my skull was several inches shorter than that of others, which meant that I was inferior. How well do I still remember my feelings when I stood there while the teacher measured my head. At first I was terribly frightened, but soon gathered up my courage when the teacher patted me on the back and said: 'There is no need to be afraid. I shall not do you any harm. After all, it is not your fault that you are inferior.' It was all nonsense, of course. What was happening was a deliberate attempt by the Nazis to give a sense of superiority to the non-Jewish majority.

The humiliation of sitting apart in lessons, of being excluded from games and ignored in the playground was too much for some children. For them, depression could turn to mental illness, even to suicide. Others, like Johnny Eichwald, fought back:

Many times I came home with a stiff lip or a black eye, until I started to learn how to box. And I remember one occasion there was a small child – he was much younger than we were. He was on his own. And he was shouting obscenities at us. I think there were four of us and we tried to have a go at him and he disappeared round the corner. But what we didn't know was that there were

about twenty of them waiting round the corner. So you
can imagine how we came home.

Such was the worry and fear of Jewish families that
many now started thinking seriously about getting
out of Germany to settle elsewhere. But this was
not easy. Germany's economic problems, including heavy unemployment, were shared by other
European countries and America. The last thing
any government wanted was a huge intake of
German refugees, who would either become
dependent on the state or, even worse in some
eyes, compete successfully for the few jobs that
were on offer. In international circles, there was
much talk of finding an undeveloped part of the
world where Jews could settle and create their own
society. New Mexico, remote and unspoiled, was
one possibility, but there were many other sugges-
tions as to where refugees could be sent, ranging
from central Africa to northern Australia. All these
ideas were so much fantasy and, anyway, beyond
the scope of any nation or nations to organize at
short notice.

The only real prospect for a Jewish homeland

was Palestine, part of which was later to become Israel. The idea of a national home for the Jewish people in Palestine had been debated for some time. In 1917, towards the end of the First World War, Britain, as the strongest power involved in the Middle East, had recognized the historical links of the Jewish people with Palestine and had given support to creating a national Jewish home. But this was not a policy that found favour with the Arab communities who were already settled there. In an attempt to avoid clashes between Arabs and Jews, Britain put a limit on the number of Jews who were permitted to emigrate to Palestine. The most that Britain was ready to allow in was just forty thousand a year. But the Jewish population in Germany was over half a million.

In 1938, a new sense of urgency came when the Nazis invaded neighbouring Austria. Almost immediately, ordinary life was made impossible for two hundred thousand Austrian Jews. Vienna became a city of fear and destitution. The risks of breaking the law were endless. 'No Jews Here' signs were everywhere. Cafes and cinemas carried warnings: 'Gypsies and Jews Keep Out'; children were told to stay away from public parks; a little girl who was brave enough to attend school found 'Cursed be the Jew' scrawled across her desk. Magda Chadwick recalls her mother having to stand in front of her shop with a placard: 'Jews must not buy or come in here'.

The man in charge of making Austria 'free of Jews' was a thirty-two-year-old Nazi fanatic called Adolf Eichmann. A cold and ruthless operator, he did all he could to make their lives unbearable. Thousands went to the *Kultusgemeinde*, the central Jewish organization, begging for visas so that they could leave Austria. Outside the United States embassy in Vienna, the queue stretched for a quarter of a mile, day and night, as people tried to get visas to emigrate to the USA. In London, the Jewish Refugees Committee received up to a thousand calls a day. But there were not enough visas to go round. With widespread economic hardship, no country wanted to open its doors to thousands of refugees.

Events in Germany brought the refugee crisis to a head. In October 1938, a group of Polish Jews living in Germany was forced back across the border into Poland. Among those deported were the parents of seventeen-year-old Herschel Grynszpan, who was hiding out as an illegal immigrant in Paris. On 7 November, Herschel made his way to the German embassy with the intention of assassinating the ambassador. Instead, he shot a high-ranking Nazi party official, Ernst von Rath, who died two days later.

The Nazi leadership took its revenge. In a single night two hundred and sixty-seven German synagogues were destroyed, thousands of Jewish shops and homes devastated, one hundred Jews murdered and many thousands arrested. This was *Kristallnacht* – the night of broken glass – when, according to one observer, anything of any Jewish value, down to the last teacup, was liable to be smashed.

Helga Kreiner was just eleven at the time of *Kristallnacht*:

When we heard the Nazi boots tramping along the street, stopping at the main front door of the block of flats where we lived, banging on the door – my mother hurriedly put out all the lights and hid with us in the corner of a bedroom. The boots tramped up the stairs, gruff voices, while our hearts beat faster and faster, the boots still tramping, halting for a moment's agonizing silence outside our front door, and then going up the next flight to the flat above . . . We heard the next morning that the gentleman who lived there, also a Jew, had been arrested. This time, they had passed us by.

Lorraine Sulzbacher lived in Fürth in Bavaria, a town with a large Jewish population. Her parents thought of themselves as Germans first and Jews second – until Hitler's arrival. On *Kristallnacht*:

I remember being woken up at one o'clock in the morning. Two Brownshirts [the uniform favoured by Hitler's followers] were running about in our flat. My mother was crying. We were told to dress. I remember walking to a square in the town and being assembled there with lots and lots of people we knew. Many were crying. People had come from the hospital, old people. It was pandemonium. It was very frightening. It was very cold and dark. They were beating the rabbi from our town and they made him jump on the Torahs which they fetched from the synagogue.

We were there for what seemed like an awful long time and then we were taken to a theatre. We were told to sit down, men at the front by the stage and women and children at the back. We were there, I think, from daybreak. During all this time they called up men on to the stage and made them perform like animals. They had to jump over tables, over chairs. All kinds of things to make them feel silly, and if they couldn't do it they beat them.

In every town, small or large, it was the same. Fourteen-year-old Ester Friedman lived in Vienna.

My father had left early to go to the American embassy – one of many, many times – to see if there would be a possibility to get a visa to go to the States. We were anxious, the atmosphere up and down the road was electric; we did not know why but a feeling of fear pervaded the air. I stood by the window – no sight of my father – but then it happened: a crowd of brown-clad SA men, with the fearful swastika armband on their sleeves, marched down the road. I leaned out further. They entered the old people's home of the Jewish community. The windows opened and out flew books. The doors opened and out came the old people, being pushed and pulled as they could not walk quickly enough. The youths and crowds laughed at the sight. Water was brought and brushes and rags, and the old people were made to kneel and scrub the pavement. And I saw. I smelled smoke. I turned my head and looked up the road. Our synagogue was burning – bright and high the flames roared – but I heard no fire engines.

Late, late, my father came home – an old, broken man, because of what he had seen and could do nothing about.

The effect of *Kristallnacht* was not quite what the Nazis intended. The reaction in other countries was one of horror and revulsion. Public opinion was at last waking up. Help had to be given to the refugees. One idea was a rescue plan for children. That something of the sort was needed was clear to anyone who read the small ads in the daily newspapers.

Please help me to bring out of Berlin two children
(boy and girl - 10 years, best family) - very
urgent case.

Which family would like to take over Jewish boy,
15 years, from first-class orthodox Viennese
family and give him the chance to be taught a
trade? (Father was in the jewellery trade, now
penniless.) Very urgent. Pocket money and clothes
will be provided.

Sympathizers came together to set up the Refugee
Children's Movement. The British government
agreed to help. From now on young refugees
would be allowed into Britain just as long as they
could be supported by friends or relations.
Moreover, a special travel document removed the
need for passports or visas. The way was clear for
the start of what was to become known as the
Kindertransporte.

Chapter Two

Escape!

The *Kindertransport* – meaning 'children's transport' –
was the name given to the rescue operation that
was to save thousands of young lives. But there
were many problems to overcome. It was one thing
for Britain to agree to take in refugee children from
Germany, but quite another to set up the organization needed to carry out the task. The first
problem was travel. Sending the children by boat
from one of the German ports was the easiest
solution. Some of the earliest arrivals did, in fact,
come on one of the luxury liners that sailed from
Hamburg, stopping off in Southampton, England,

before going on to America. However, although the Nazis were keen to get rid of their Jewish citizens, after *Kristallnacht* they were sensitive to international opinion: refugee ships crowded with children would not look good on the front pages of the foreign press. They thought it would be better if the children were transported by train. In this way, it would be easier to fix the place and time of departure to avoid unfavourable publicity. But a train to where? In the days long before the Channel Tunnel, there was no direct route to Britain.

At first it was thought that the best way was across the German border into France, and from there by ferry from one of the Channel ports. Unfortunately, the French government was reluctant to get involved. There was better news from Holland. Not only were there extensive rail links with Germany, but the Dutch government was sympathetic to the refugee cause. From Amsterdam came a promise of cooperation, including hostel accommodation for those children who for some reason were held up at the border.

Having decided on the main route for the *Kindertransporte* – by train to the Hook of Holland,

and boat to the port of Harwich in England – the next priority was to choose the passengers. Inevitably, selection was haphazard, often depending on knowing the right people or being in the right place at the right time. Half the two hundred or so children on the first *Kindertransport* were from a Berlin orphanage destroyed on *Kristallnacht*. Another forty were children of Polish descent, who had been told to leave Germany. The rest were young people whose parents were in concentration camps.

On 1 December 1938, refugee children started gathering at Berlin's main railway station. The hours before departure were spent deciding what to wear and what clothing to pack, what childhood treasures to take along (there was a warning that anything of resale value, like jewellery and cameras, would be confiscated) and what to eat on the train. Each child was allowed one suitcase. Parents had strange ideas about the sort of clothing that would match British fashion sense – thick tweed was favoured for boys, who were dressed up to look like young Sherlock Holmeses. Richard Grunberger recalls:

My mother bought me an outfit which marked me as a complete foreigner as soon as I arrived in England. I had a pleated jacket and tight-fitting trousers, which I soon came to know as plus fours. But, though I felt strange, I didn't worry too much about it at the time. I was too concerned about the shop owner. He had a badge on his lapel that showed that he was a long-serving Nazi.

The bolder parents set their imaginations to work on ways to get round the restrictions on taking anything of value out of the country. A few boys carried new Leica cameras, which they hoped to sell in England, but other ruses were more subtle. It was not entirely to support his musical talent that Leslie Brent's mother gave him a violin. Stringed instruments held their worth and could fetch good prices.

Yoash Kahn was nervous that someone would show interest in the contents of his washbag.

I had been given a medallion – the sort you wear on a chain round your neck. It had my initials on one side and some Hebrew letters on the other. My parents were determined that I should take it with me, so one of them got a tin of Nivea cream, peeled off the silver paper-covering very carefully, buried the medallion in the cream and then resealed the tin. Of course, I was scared out of my wits the whole journey. I'm the sort of person who never takes anything through customs illegally because I just know that my face will give me away. But somehow I managed to get away with this. I remember, I couldn't quite believe it, and for days after arriving in London I kept the medallion in the Nivea, checking every now and then that it was still there.

Most parents played by the rules. The consequences of being found out were too grim to contemplate. Told not to take any money, Henry Toch left with three pfennigs in his pocket: 'My first contact with the English was begging for a penny to send a card home.'

The constant warning from parents was to be polite to the SS guards – members of the special military police force, who themselves acted as if they were beyond the law. Sometimes it paid off. When Felix Hunter was asked by a tight-lipped guard: 'Where are you going?' he replied, almost apologetically: 'To England.' The frown turned to a smile. 'Oh, you'll enjoy it there. I wish I was going.'

Other parents were all for braving it out. The parting words to Nina Liebermann were shouted by her mother across a crowded platform: 'And if they ask for your gold earrings at the frontier, just take them off and throw them out of the window.'

As the time came for leaving, parents and children suffered conflicting emotions – sadness, excitement, fear, relief. Dorothy Sim practised her English:

All I succeeded in learning was 'I want to go to the WC', which my parents and I in our ignorance pronounced 'VK,' and 'I have a handkerchief in my pocket'. Among my clothes they packed a box full of precious family photographs, my own set of cutlery and a toilet case with cloth and soap. My father had taken the toilet case with him when he fought in the First World War. He had won the Iron Cross.

I recall arriving at the railway station in Hamburg. There were two stone lions guarding the entrance. I was carrying my toy dog, Droll, and I had my leather shoulder bag on. I dropped Droll underneath the train and a man had to climb down and rescue him. I had a peach and a pear in my shoulder bag. We children boarded the train to get our places. Then I was sent off again to say farewell to my mother and father. I can see them to this day. They were standing in a corridor behind a barrier. I said my goodbyes and then walked back up the long corridor away from them and into the train.

Leslie Brent was seen off by his parents and his sister:

My mother was very tearful but my father put on a stiff upper lip. To me it all seemed very bewildering. It is hard to describe my feelings. I was low but not utterly desolate because I realized that all this was being done for my good. I was aware of the fact that some great act of kindness had been extended to me. Certainly I had no idea that I would not go back again or that my family would die. That is something I couldn't have foreseen and I don't think anyone did.

It was the same feeling of perplexity for Hans Groschler, now Herbert Gale. With his younger brother, he travelled from his home town in Friesland to Berlin.

Our father took us; Mother preferred not to come. I remember that I did not find it too distressing because I had been moving around the country for the past two or three years, from one Jewish school to another. Father dropped us off at the collecting point and he stayed in a hotel. The next morning when we went to the authorities to collect our papers, I was beginning to feel apprehensive and sad. On the second morning my father took us to the train. We said our goodbyes and promised to write often. I was very bewildered and I could not fully understand what was going on.

Celia Lee came from Hamburg to Britain. She was recovering from appendicitis when she was told she had been accepted for the first Kindertransport. Soon after the war, when she was still a teenager, she wrote about her experiences:

For my twelve years I was hearing and learning too much lately. The hospital was a Jewish one. Half the male doctors had been sent to the concentration camp.

Earlier Mummy had whispered to me that Daddy was in hiding. It did not make sense. Dad was no criminal.

Nurse was helping me get dressed so that Daddy would not have to wait for me. When he came in I cried and hugged him ever so tightly. Secretly I had been worried, but seeing him reassured me that things were not too bad. When I had finished telling him all the news I had been saving, he held me gently and said, 'How would you like to go to Holland or England, chatterbox?' I stared at him. 'Do you mean it? Is Max coming too? Why are we going? Are you and Mummy coming too?'

My father looked at me gravely. 'You are old enough to understand. A lot has happened while you have been in hospital. Things aren't the same for Jewish people. It would be safer for you and Max to go to another country. Mummy and I will follow later, if we can.'

'Let's go to England then.' I had made up my mind, thinking of the two years' English I had learned at school. And my brother, Max, would be coming; that meant a lot to me.

That was on the Sunday. On Thursday we left for England. The days between flowed by. There was shopping to be done and papers to be put in order. A big red 'J' was stamped on the front of my passport. I was so excited, I did not notice the tired and strained expressions on my parents' faces.

When we said goodbye, I did not burst into tears. I was just so sure in my own mind that we would see one another again soon. Mummy gave me a golden necklace and Daddy gave me a lucky money piece to hang on the necklace. For the first time that week I came out of the haze I had been living in. I had a premonition that things were more serious than I had taken them to be.

The Berlin-Hamburg *Kindertransport* of 1 December 1938 showed what could be done. The entire exercise had been mounted in little more than a week and, though there were a huge number of disappointed families who failed to get places, there was the promise of more Kindertransport to come.

The first *Kindertransport* out of Vienna in Austria left on 11 December 1938. Gerta Jassem said her goodbyes in April 1938 at the Westbahnhof Station in Vienna.

My father placed the single suitcase on to the overhead rack of the compartment and then, as it was very crowded, had to step down to the platform. We children crowded round the window to receive uncertain last-minute instructions. Nothing new or really important was said. The desperate hopelessness of the people left behind was not really grasped by us.

One of Gerta's last memories of parting was her mother asking her what food she wanted:

I assumed she meant as a sort of farewell meal, so I chose my favourite dish, *Wiener schnitzel**, and I was so disappointed when I opened a brown paper bag and found instead meat patties on a roll.

Another point of issue between Gerta and her mother was the bright idea of hollowing out the heels of her daughter's walking boots.

She hid my watch, a gold bracelet and a few gold coins. This made me very conscious of my feet as I tried to

* Breaded escalope of veal

walk nonchalantly in laced-up boots while feeling scared that someone would notice.

There was some comfort in journeying by train. It was a closed world in which the children could take strength from knowing that they were all part of the same mad plot. Gerta Jassem shared a compartment with seven other girls and boys aged between six and thirteen, all strangers to each other.

We ate our sandwiches, exchanged stories, told jokes. The monotonous rhythm of the train made us sleepy. I remember putting my head on my arms and leaning forward on to the folded table in front of my seat. The next girl rested on my back and this started a sort of chain reaction of bodies. We woke up whenever the train stopped, and when we were at a station we got out for a while. Then there was lots of shouting from one track to another before we started again. We had no idea where we were, though we thought we had crossed from Austria into Germany. It was next morning before one of the supervisors came to tell us that we were near the Dutch border.

This was the moment when regrets at parting from family and friends were suppressed by the fear of being sent back.

Two uniformed, brown-booted Germans, one wearing the SS insignia, entered our compartment. They pointed at the suitcases they wanted opened. They never uttered a word and nor did we. We simply watched and tried to look unconcerned as they searched our cases. There was a rumour that if just one of the group was discovered smuggling money or jewellery, the whole transport would be sent back. Finally, they left the train and we saw them standing in groups on the platform.

It was only when the train started moving that we began to relax. As we gathered speed, someone shouted: 'Look, we're in no-man's-land!' Somehow, the countryside did look different; less ordered perhaps, or maybe there were just more houses. Anyway, what did it matter? We jumped about, cheered and sang. We opened the windows wide and held out our handkerchiefs, scarves and jackets to wave at the deserted fields.

Of those who had crossed the border a few days earlier on the Berlin-Hamburg *Kindertransport*, Nina

Liebermann and her sister were less nervous of the SS guards than of the adult passengers who were sharing their compartment. Everyone was so much on edge, the girls were sure they were not alone in having something to hide.

We stopped for customs inspection on the German side. I tried to look unconcerned as the cases were searched. I was certain I would lose my earrings. But they left us alone. Suddenly the train started to move, first slowly, then gathering speed for a short way before stopping again. Two men in uniform appeared in our compartment. I was sure they had come back for my earrings. But how could that be? It dawned on me that they were Dutch border guards. They went over to a conservatively dressed passenger in a corner seat and asked him to go with them. He did not come back. We heard later that a German spy had been caught.

Johnny Blunt was less fortunate in his encounter with German customs.

I was very proud of my stamp collection which I kept in my rucksack. An SA man found it and put it on the seat beside me while he started searching someone else. When his back was turned I took the stamp album and sat on it. He must have realized because he turned and gave me a smack across the face. He took the stamp album and told me: 'You can start another collection when you're in England.'

The tension was increased by the sight of German troops massed along the Dutch frontier. Kurt Weinburg recalls:

The train stood for a long, long time at the border. I watched from the window as German soldiers marched up and down. They were nothing to do with us; they were just drilling. But there was a tremendous sense of relief when we got into the Dutch station.

The contrast between the sullen dismissal by the Nazi guards and the welcome from the Dutch refugee workers could not have been greater. All along the platform were smiling women with trolleys loaded with food. They handed out cakes and sandwiches and chocolate, and offered lemonade drinks. If there was time in hand or the train was held up, the children were treated to huge meals of meat and beans. Presents and games added to the party atmosphere. Years on, many a *Kindertransport* girl would not be parted from the rag doll pressed into her arms by a total stranger on a Dutch railway station.

The frantic activity in Berlin, Vienna and at the Dutch border to keep up the flow of child refugees was matched in London by efforts to make the journey worthwhile. This responsibility was carried by the Refugee Children's Movement, an organization of chiefly unpaid volunteers who had offices in central London close to the British Museum. It was their job to identify likely foster parents who, at their own expense or with a small allowance, would be ready to welcome one or more children into their homes. A radio appeal brought in offers of support, but it took time for the RCM to check out accommodation. Preparations were still in hand when children on the first *Kindertransport* were filing on-board the *De Praag*, docked at the Hook of Holland.

For those brought up in central Germany, it

was often their first encounter with the sea. The experience was not encouraging. The crossing from the Hook to Harwich can be rough at any time of year, but in the winter of 1938 it was like riding a rollercoaster. Nina Liebermann was lucky enough to be a good sailor. Not so her younger sister, Ella:

> She became violently seasick and for the next couple of hours I had to hold her head over the railing, all the while bathing her face with eau de cologne. (To this day, the very smell of it makes my sister feel ill.) When, at last, her bouts of seasickness subsided, I sank down exhausted on to our luggage in the cabin hold of the boat. The next thing I knew was someone pinching my cheeks and saying: 'Don't worry. She can't be dead with rosy cheeks like that.' When I opened my eyes, my sister was staring at me, her lips quivering. I don't think I have ever slept so soundly. But it was my first rest in more than twenty-four hours.

Coming from Hamburg, thirteen-year-old Gerd Nathan had lived close to the North Sea. But this was his first crossing.

On the boat we were two to a cabin and I occupied the top bunk. It must have been one of the roughest nights, it was terrible, and it was the one and only time I have been seasick. The chap below me was sick and that of course triggered me off. But I do recall after being sick I was very hungry and I had my favourite sandwiches in my coat pocket (sardine sandwiches – sandwiches in oil!) and I wanted them. But I was so weak I couldn't get off the bunk to get them and the boy below was too weak as well.

The first thing I did on arriving in England was to have my sardine sandwiches – I was very hungry.

(For those who could face up to a meal on arrival in England, there was a first hint that English people and English ways might be, well, somehow different. Milk in tea was thought to be a curious habit and there was some consternation at the sight of square, thin slices of white bread. Alfred Cooper assumed he was being offered cake, but thought how crazy it was to eat it with butter. Up to then he had been used to thick slices of rye bread.)

The *De Praag* docked at Parkeston Quay at five-thirty in the morning of Friday, 2 December 1938.

By six o'clock the children were ready for their first encounter with the British families who were to take them in. A reporter from the *Eastern Daily Press* observed the scene:

As each child filed through the ship's lounge, which had been turned into a temporary office, an official 'labelled' him or her. 'Hans Jacobus,' somebody called out. A youth stepped forward, took off his cap, and a woman tied around his neck an ordinary luggage label, on which was scratched his number and name. 'Manfred Landau . . . Hella Richter . . .' and so the disembarkation went on.

Never has a sadder boatload of passengers filed through the customs barriers at Harwich. As the officers patted their pockets, trying to put the children at their ease with smiles and words of broken German, some of them timorously emptied their pockets, and there was laid out on the long table an odd assortment of fountain pens, propelling pencils, cheap flash lamps and schoolboy odds and ends – their only possessions apart from the clothes they wore and the few garments stuffed in the rucksacks.

Another reporter detected a more cheerful mood.

Full of excitement at visiting a strange land, the children showed little effect of their long journey and rough crossing, or indeed of the modern tragedy in which they have been involved.

It was more likely that the bland smiles were a thin disguise for total bewilderment. Few had any English; they could only guess at what was being said to them. Helga Samuel was not alone in fearing the worst.

Perhaps because I looked more lost and sad than the other children, I was picked out by a photographer who came over to me and said something which of course I did not understand. I began to cry so he put his arm round my shoulder and gave me a coin (I later found out it was a half-a-crown*). Then he called over one of the helpers and, with her looking at the label round my neck, he took our picture.

* A half-a-crown: a coin worth two shillings and sixpence – 12.5p today!

In the last month before war was declared, families who were still on the waiting list for places on the *Kindertransporte*, but knew they had little chance of moving up the queue, took to waiting at the main railway stations, watching and hoping.

Seven-year-old Sonia Altman had a foster parent in Middlesbrough but, having missed one transport date because she had to have her tonsils out, there seemed little prospect of an early escape from Vienna.

My mother was getting desperate. So every day, she packed my case and we haunted the station. I was getting quite used to these trips, me in my best clothes with a little label saying who I was and where I was going. Then, on 13 June, we were standing by a crowded train when we saw a mother who was in a dreadful state. She just couldn't bear to part with her child and at the last moment held her back. My mother took her chance and literally threw me on to the train. The doors were slammed and off I went. I remember holding my doll and crying all the time. I wanted my mother but of course she wasn't there any more.

A despairing mother, spotting a thirteen-year-old boy seated by an open window, thrust her infant into his arms. The train pulled out. He looked after the little girl throughout the journey, everyone, including the Gestapo guards, assuming that it was his sister nestling in his lap. He held on to his charge until he came off the boat at Harwich. To this day, he wonders how she made out.

On the German side there were still efforts to avoid bad publicity. Greater use was made of quiet sub-urban stations or of quieter platforms on the main stations; trains left at night and the number of family wellwishers coming to say goodbye was restricted to one parent for each child. The new rules were self-defeating. To load up a *Kindertransport* in lonely isolation was to attract more, not less, attention.

Vera Coppard left Berlin in May 1939 when she was thirteen.

Mother couldn't bear to come to the station. I went with my father. There was a terrible scene when they were shouting out the names of the children. There was one woman who was very agitated and when her children were not on the list she became hysterical. The guards hit her with clubs and knocked her to the ground. Then we were handed on to the platform. I just had time to say goodbye to father. My former nanny managed to get on to the platform, I don't know how. She threw oranges through the carriage window.

The journey was terrible. At stations all along the way, parents had gathered to catch a last glimpse of their children. I'm glad my family didn't do that.

The port of Harwich in England brings much happier memories – a favourite being the policeman who actually smiled. 'It was then that I made up my mind that I would never leave England,' declares Lotte Bray from Lowenstein. 'A country where a policeman smiled had to be a good place to settle.'

There were the inevitable difficulties with English. Johnny Blunt could only say 'yes, no, door, window', but he did better than Harold Waterman (Hans Wasserman) who knew a complete sentence: 'The gardener's in the garden.' Harold waited thirty years to use it in conversation.

The last of the *Kindertransporte* to leave Germany before the start of the war steamed out on 31 August 1939. It was a close-run thing. Just hours before the train was scheduled to depart, a call came through to London, warning that the transport was about to be cancelled. With the threat of war ever closer, the Dutch decided to close the border, which meant that the train would be stuck in Germany. It was pointless even to start the journey. But after much persuasion, the Dutch authorities gave way. The train would be allowed to cross the border if it was guaranteed that the children would be taken on to Britain. The train left on time, though with fewer children than expected. There were places for sixty-six passengers but, as the train was boarding, the total was cut to sixty. The youngest were left behind. The last *Kindertransport* made it to the boat waiting at the Hook of Holland, which sailed in the early hours of 1 September 1939, two days before war was declared.

Chapter Three

New Experiences

For those children who had foster parents or relatives waiting for them, the next stop after Harwich was London. A reception centre, run by the Refugee Children's Movement, was set up under one of the railway arches at Liverpool Street station. When a train of refugee children arrived it was met by volunteer helpers, mostly well-to-do young women who could afford to throw themselves into charity work. One of these was Elaine Blond, the youngest daughter of Michael Marks (of the famous Marks & Spencer), who recalls the muddle and confusion.

When the train pulled into Liverpool Street there was always a line of people waiting on the platform. In front were the families who had offered to take in a child and who were eager to catch a first glimpse of their boy or girl. They were inevitably anxious, wondering perhaps, at this critical moment, if they had been too reckless with their hospitality, or simply worried about getting over the awkwardness of introductions. One mother told me she was so nervous that when it came to the point she could not remember the name of the boy she was meeting. I am sure that many of the children suffered the same problem in reverse.

However well-meaning, there were those who could behave with dreadful insensitivity – by letting the disappointment show when the flaxen-haired beauty of their dreams turned out to be a tiny tub with pimples.

Once in the hall, the children were led to seats and the process of identification began. Many in the crowd of foster parents soon got fed up with waiting.

'I don't see why I can't take her now. I'm her auntie, aren't I? Look, here are the papers, Schmitt is the name.

I am Mrs Schmitt and Elsa Schmitt is my own husband's brother Max's only child!'

'Yes, yes. I understand. But please, would you mind waiting just a little while!'

Eventually the RCM lady with the loudest voice had to climb on a chair and appeal for order. 'Please remain behind the barrier until you are called. I will now read the list of names. When you hear your name, please come forward to the table where you can sign the papers and take your child.'

Only the children with a smattering of English had any idea what was going on. Pacified by what was now a familiar handout of a packet of sandwiches, some chocolate and an orange, the rest, like ten-year-old Angela Carpos, were bewildered.

The room was awesome; cold and grey. And I had a problem. I wanted to go to the loo but I didn't dare ask. My name was called and I was given to Mr Littlejohn, who couldn't speak a word of German. I couldn't speak a word of English. He proceeded to take me round London. He wanted to buy things at shops. I said no. I was well brought up and didn't accept presents. All I wanted was to go to the loo. Eventually he took me to a Lyons Corner House. He put two pennies into my hand (I had never seen a penny) and sent me upstairs. I went into the washroom but couldn't work out how to open the door to the toilet. I went to an attendant and, trying to be polite, said '*Hände waschen*' and mimed washing my hands. The stupid woman took my penny, gave me a towel and put me in front of a basin.

When the foster parent was a relative or friend, the first reaction after the hugs and kisses was to take hold of the label round the child's neck, tear it off and throw it to the ground. The gesture was entirely understandable.

With strangers, things were taken more slowly. Dorli and Lieserl Oppenheimer were met by the Lersky family, friends of their parents. Mrs Lersky reported back to Vienna on the day's events:

On Thursday at three o'clock we were all at the station with thumping hearts. Punctually at three o'clock the train drew in and it was very moving how all the small and big children streamed out; there were surely none on that platform who didn't have tears in their eyes. I worked my way through all the scenes of greeting and then quickly found both of ours, waiting very nicely, hand in hand.

Of course there was a frightful commotion and it was a bit difficult to get to the processing point. Dorli naturally composed herself very well but the little one was still very tired. We stowed them in a taxi and at home they were quickly refreshed and the little one was immediately put to bed, where she soon dropped off to sleep peacefully. At this time, as always, your 'big' daughter showed such touching selflessness and such motherliness to the little one, one could only be amazed. When Lieserl was already in bed, Dorli was still in her coat and could not be moved to think of herself. I have never seen such a thing in a ten-year-old. Everyone was full of praise for her.

Even when relatives were on hand, the first critical days could be very disorganized, as Kurt Weinburg can confirm:

At Liverpool Street station my aunt collected me. The plan was for me to go to a hostel, but for some reason it wasn't ready. Suddenly there was a panic and accommodation had to be found. My aunt knew a family who had come to England a few months before, from Düsseldorf, who were planning to open an old folk's home for German refugees near Lewisham. She asked them if they could give me shelter until the hostel was ready. That's how I came to spend my first night in an empty house on a camp bed. I arrived on a Thursday and on the Sunday I wanted to visit my uncle and aunt in Putney. I went on a train via Waterloo. I had written out everything I had to say in English – I was very nervous.

Real fear came to those who thought they were abandoned. Barely able to speak English, adrift in a strange country, Nina Liebermann could find no trace of Mrs Landers who was supposed to be at the station.

None of the women I approached answered to that name. My sister could not walk any more. Looking back, I saw her fall asleep on top of the luggage. All the other children had, by then, been met and spirited away. Desperately, I made another sweep of the now almost empty platform. I spotted a comfortable-looking woman, who seemed also to be on a search operation. I went up to her. 'Yes, I'm Mrs Landers. Where have you been? I've been looking for you for at least two hours. You should have arrived at nine o'clock.'

At the end of it, there were always some children left over – those who had come on the wrong day or, more frequently, whose sponsors had muddled the date.

It was mostly the teenagers who were hardest to place with families. Those who were ready to be foster parents usually had in mind a child who was aged ten or under. But the early transports included fifteen to nineteen-year-olds who were eager to get out of Germany because they had been threatened with imprisonment if they stayed.

Desperately searching for temporary homes for their young guests, the RCM hit on the idea of taking over two holiday camps: one at Dovercourt, a small Essex seaside resort just along the coast from Harwich, the other further away at Pakefield, near Lowestoft. Out of season, the camps were unoccupied and cheap to rent.

Dovercourt in the 1930s was an Essex coastal village favoured by those who enjoyed stiff breezes and bracing walks. From the seafront up to a mile inland was an uninterrupted expanse of tall grass and fern, the delight of ramblers. But in the wet months it could turn into a marshland. It was the wide, open spaces that had appealed to Billy Butlin, one of the pioneers of holidays for working families. At a Butlin's holiday camp, everything was laid on, but at bargain rates. Mum and Dad could relax knowing that the children were being looked after, that someone else was cooking the meals and that every evening would bring some form of entertainment. There was a communal dining hall, children's play areas between the fir trees and lines of tiny chalets or miniature bungalows. But there was no heating because this wasn't strictly essential in the summer months. The problem for the RCM was that they were taking over the camp at the beginning of one of the coldest winters on record.

When the first *Kindertransport* arrived at Dovercourt, it was cold but dry. The children's immediate reaction was a sense of relief at having arrived somewhere. Then there was the excitement of finding out about this strange miniature town with its open view of the North Sea over the mud flats.

Celia Lee's first impression of Dovercourt was roses. 'I couldn't believe it: roses in wintertime! It made a strong impact on me. What a beautiful country.' Others remember the green of the countryside. 'The first question they asked,' reported a voluntary worker, 'was, "May we go on the grass?" They were astonished when we said, "Yes."' Everyone remembers the holiday chalets – 'our little houses' as they were soon to be called.

There was curiosity and wonderment at those features of life that seemed so strange to those not brought up in Britain – like porridge and kippers for breakfast, 'a peculiar liquid which looked like coffee, tasted like poison and was said to be tea', and bottles of HP Sauce and vinegar on the dining table.

Stone hot-water bottles were a puzzle; so too were blankets instead of duvets ('I had always associated blankets with picnics, holidays and Wild West stories'), and English toilet paper ('hard and shiny'). The new experience everyone enjoyed was eating bananas and it was a great disappointment when the supply stopped at the beginning of the war. Also missed was German sausage, made more intense for one boy who had brought a whole salami all the way from Vienna only to have it thrown away by a Dovercourt helper 'because it didn't smell right'.

A reporter from the *Jewish Chronicle* visiting Dovercourt a week after the arrival of the first *Kindertransport* had nothing but praise for the RCM.

Everybody I saw was dressed in the warmest clothes . . . and all the children are given plenty of blankets to keep them warm at night . . . Some were playing table tennis, some darts (it was amusing to watch their efforts at this game, which was entirely new to them) . . . In a side room there were several surrounding a piano, which was being played by a youngster of about ten.

But it did not take a sharp journalistic instinct to realize that for refugees – particularly young refugees – life could never be that simple.

Closer observation here revealed a group of three little girls, one with a doll clutched to her, seated quite silently in a corner, and there a boy rubbing his eyes furtively.

In the weeks ahead, the loneliness would intensify, but in the early days there was enough happening to keep homesickness at bay. A stream of visitors turned up at the camp, among them the local MP, the mayor of Harwich and the chief rabbi, all with words of encouragement and the promise of better things to come.

For Celia Lee the excitement of meeting new people soon wore off. She recorded her impressions of Dovercourt in 1941.

All day long we had no peace. At first it was fun, but afterwards we got tired of standing, jumping, dancing and sitting, of talking to and shaking hands with more or less important people from the district.

For the first time in its history, Dovercourt was news. Though some newspapers were critical of handing out charity to foreigners, the general line was to stress the benefits of taking in such 'lively, sturdily built and intelligent' children. *Picture Post* thought the young refugees would be a credit to Britain:

> They will be trained . . . to become farmers and farm-workers, artisans, plumbers, builders, electricians. Many of the girls will become nurses, maids or farm assistants.

Of all the journalists who visited Dovercourt, the team from the BBC caused the greatest excitement. Radio was still in its early days and the idea of putting out a half-hour programme on the child refugees – to be called *Children in Flight* – was a great piece of publicity for the RCM.

The children threw themselves into the project, telling the reporter about the good things in life while diplomatically forgetting the not so good. Their chief spokesman was Leslie Brent, who was chosen for his sound grasp of English. The words came over clearly but cautiously:

> A bell rings at eight o'clock and we have to get up. Some boys get up earlier to make a run to the sea which is near the camp. At eight-thirty we have a good English

breakfast, which we enjoy. First we did not eat porridge but now we like it. When we finish the breakfast we get the letters or cards from our parents, and then we are all very happy. After that we clear and tidy our rooms, then we have two hours' lessons in English. When the lessons are over we take our lunch and then we can make what we like. After tea we can go to the sea, which is wonderful, or we play English games of football. In the evening we learn a lot of English songs till we go to bed. I sleep with two other boys in a nice little house. Now it is very cold and we cannot stay in our house. We like to sit around the stove in a very large hall, and we read or write to our parents. The people are very kind to us. A gentleman invited me to go with him in a car; then we drove to his house and there we had tea. Oh, it was very nice. Sometimes we go to a picture house in Dovercourt. We have seen the good film *Snow White and the Seven Dwarfs*. We were all delighted. Now I will go to school, then I can speak English good and then I would like to become a cook. We are all very happy to be in England.

Leslie Brent was denied his ambition to be a cook. Instead, he became a professor of immunology, but says that he still enjoys cooking.

In the last weeks of December, the refugee camp at Pakefield had to be evacuated because of the severe cold. Two hundred and fifty children were moved to a girls' school in Southwold, where the staff gave up their holiday to help look after their guests. The luxury of single cubicles and warm beds lasted until the end of the first week in January when the regular boarders returned. Then it was back to Lowestoft and a new set of problems.

After the snow came the rain. One night the water in the gullies flooded over into the chalets. Children were carried shoulder-high to the road, where a bus took them to a seafront hotel. They spent the night sleeping on the ballroom floor. After that it was boys only at Pakefield. The girls went to Dovercourt. Not that conditions there were very much better. The chalets on the lower ground nearest the beach were liable to flood and more than once young children had to be lifted from their beds in the middle of the night. On these occasions a dormitory was improvised in the dining room.

Early in the new year, Anna Essinger, an experienced head teacher, was asked to take charge of the welfare and education of all children at Dovercourt and Pakefield. Having emigrated from Germany with most of her school some five years earlier, she and her staff knew a thing or two about the traumas of young people settling in a strange country. Anna Essinger did not like what she found at Dovercourt.

One of her immediate problems was over-crowding. Dovercourt was designed for five hundred residents at most, but was providing for up to twice as many. Those children leaving the camp to go to foster parents (about one hundred in December) were vastly outnumbered by new arrivals.

The call went out for teaching assistants. Train fares and free board and lodging were offered, plus pocket money 'where necessary', but this was never more than a pound a week. Vera Tann's husband, Fred, was a railway shipping clerk at Parkeston Quay continental office. When he told his wife about the children at Dovercourt she and a friend went along to help teach English.

We put everyday articles on a table, sat around and taught them to ask: 'What is this?' – a spoon, fork, knife, sugar, milk and, later, because they watched the workmen, a saw, hammer, screws, nails. It was all a game but they learned very fast.

Another volunteer spent her first evening at Dovercourt simply observing the children.

Some of the older children are talking round one of the stoves, a few of the younger ones have toys to play with and there are always groups round the ping pong tables. Very few are reading, partly because it is difficult for these children to concentrate after all the excitement of their journey and arrival in a strange country, and partly because the books which have been presented to the camp are nearly all English. But there is one occupation that is unfailingly popular among them all, no matter what their age, and that is writing letters.

She forgot to mention the noise. Everybody else remembers the uproar in what was known grandly as the Palm Court, the former bar and dance hall, where several lessons were held simultaneously during the day. Classes gathered round the pipe stoves which gave out a strong smell of soot. Much fun was had learning the popular English songs of the time: 'Tipperary', 'Underneath the Spreading Chestnut Tree', 'Daisy, Daisy' and the 'Lambeth Walk' – simple, rousing tunes.

The radio programme *Children in Flight* was broadcast on the evening of 3 January 1939. Gladys Rushbrook heard the programme at her home in Leigh-on-Sea. Her husband had just finished the day's work at his butcher's shop and they were settling down to supper.

It was so terribly sad; we felt surely there was something we could do. So we decided that at the weekend we would go to Dovercourt to see the children and find out if we could help in any way.

We were introduced to four boys, all of about seventeen. Each Sunday we used to go to Dovercourt and take them for a ride in the country and then to Clacton, where we had tea before bringing them back to the camp.

Parcels of food and clothing started arriving at Dovercourt. There were shoes and coats from

Marks & Spencer; the National Sporting Club sent a pair of boxing gloves and an Essex butcher provided beef sausages for all, once a week. Free tickets at the Harwich Electric Cinema provided a welcome diversion from camp routine, not to mention a painless method of learning English. News of Dovercourt travelled abroad. One day a trunk-load of winter woollens turned up, a gift from Johannesburg, South Africa, where a news item in the local paper had inspired a ladies' circle to start knitting.

But however welcome, such generosity did not help solve the central problem which was to find suitable homes for the children. Every Sunday, prospective foster parents gathered at Dovercourt to view the inmates. It was a ritual that distressed Anna Essinger but, given the pressure to move the children out of the camp so that others could take their places, nobody was able to come up with a better alternative to what was known as 'the market'.

Sunday was the day for looking smart. For three hours in the morning the dining room became a barber's shop, with a queue of youngsters waiting for their short back and sides. Baths were mandatory and not just a lazy soaking, but a good scrubbing with carbolic soap. Then the best clothes were chosen, none of them the height of fashion nor even necessarily a good fit, but neat, tidy and clean.

The adults were told to arrive when the children were having lunch. That way, by walking between the long tables as if on a tour of inspection, they could view the prospects without embarrassment. Anyway, that was the theory. In reality, adults and children usually ended up furtively edging round each other, anxiously trying to detect matching personalities.

In the evening, the names of those who had been picked from the line-up were read out over the camp tannoy. The children were apprehensive, none more so than the newcomers, who were still struggling with their English and were generally mystified by events. When Zita Hirschhorn heard her name, so little acquainted was she with all that was going on, she cried out: '*Ich bin verkauft*' ('I am sold').

The greatest sadness was the children who felt

unwanted. These were not necessarily the shy or reserved ones, who were quite likely to be snapped up by 'parents' who were looking for a quiet life. But a child who was unusual in some way – a thin, undernourished-looking boy, for example, or a large, overnourished-looking girl – were liable to feel the pain of rejection. It was said that the teenagers were the most difficult to manage. But who could blame them? Exiled from their own country through no fault of their own, they resented stern reminders not to speak German, to be polite and always, always to be grateful. Stuck in Dovercourt with little prospect of continuing their education or of fulfilling their parents' ambitions, they did not see what they had to be grateful for.

Dovercourt ended its days as a refugee centre in March 1939, when there were less than a hundred, mostly older boys, still in occupation. For a short time, Dovercourt was restored to its original function, but in 1942 it was taken over as a prisoner-of-war camp. It was to be another five years before the holidaymakers returned.

Chapter Four

Foster Families

To qualify as the ideal foster parent you had to be fairly well off with an already established family; it helped if you lived in rural Britain (this suggested healthy living), spoke a little German, and could tolerate moody children who suffered bouts of depression and were inclined to long silences. And you had to be Jewish.

However, typical foster parents were not at all like this. Chiefly from the poorer social groups, they lived in a small house in a town or city, had no children, or had children who were grown up, spoke not a word of German, knew nothing of

Germany beyond the front-page news of the *Express* or *Mirror*, and did not begin to understand the problems of being a young refugee. And the typical foster parent was not Jewish.

Why were there not more Jewish families willing to take in refugee children? The Jews of Britain were a tiny minority, less than one per cent of the population. For the six years leading up to the war, they had raised millions of pounds to help the Jews of Germany and had absorbed over sixty thousand refugees. One reaction – 'They can afford it' – sprang from the common assumption that all Jews were well off. But anyone who was familiar with the less fashionable districts of London, Manchester and Leeds knew otherwise. The average Jew was the average Englishman, living off a weekly pay packet of four pounds a week or less at a time when, in the worst-hit areas for unemployment, up to twenty per cent of the population was living below the poverty line. Then there were those Jewish families who were unsuitable to act as foster parents, because they were too young, too old or too inexperienced, and those who simply chose not to help, even though they could afford to. It was unrealistic to expect the remaining Jewish community to absorb ten thousand refugee children.

From the day of its foundation, the RCM was committed to accepting help from whatever source. If a Christian family was willing to take in a Jewish child, then the offer was gratefully received. To have done otherwise, it was argued, would have meant turning away young refugees because there were no homes for them to go to.

Jewish or Christian, foster parents were hard to find and those who did come forward were not always of the highest quality. Ursula Cohn did not even get a good night's sleep before plunging into the realities of her new life with her foster family in North-west London:

> Unfortunately, they did not look after me very well. On the day I arrived they gave me a hot drink and after an hour I did the ironing – the ironing for the whole family, having just arrived in England . . .

Ursula was expected to do all the housework, look after the baby of the family, and was paid 2/6d (12½p) a week.

Split up from her brother, Diane Garner had no complaints about her foster mother – 'She was a very loving woman.' Her brother was less fortunate:

His foster parents were what I would call professional do-gooders. But after about four years they said they couldn't cope with him. He was expelled from school at the age of seven and they said he was destructive when in fact he just tried to find out how things worked. He'd take a watch to pieces and then couldn't put it together again. They put him in a national children's home and told my mother he was in boarding school. They washed their hands of him and my brother had terrible hang-ups for the rest of his life.

Many of the children suffered long bouts of loneliness. Manfred Drechsler remembers how much he missed his mother:

My mother and I were very close. I so loved her. She mollycoddled me. When I came to England I couldn't breathe. I was so longing for my mother. I missed her terribly. Then I cut her out of my mind. I can remember my father's face without looking at a photo, but without a photo I can't remember my mother's face.

Herbert Holzinger tried hard to keep a stiff upper lip when he was introduced, with his ten-year-old sister, to his new home:

Our first day in Birmingham was hell. It suddenly hit me that we were in a foreign country without knowing the language, without relatives or friends, and I was trying desperately to be brave, as a thirteen-year-old boy was expected to behave. I spent most of that day in and out of the toilet so that no one could see the tears rolling down my cheeks.

Martha Blend had her first sight of a new foster mother in the cavernous waiting room at Liverpool Street station:

I found myself being taken charge of by a small plump woman who spoke to me in the nearest she could get to German, which was Yiddish. She took me home to a little Victorian terraced house in Bow, East London. Her husband was an out-of-work London cabbie. As they had no children of their own they had decided to take me on. When she asked me what I wanted to do I replied with one word, *schlafen* [sleep], and was glad to sink into the bed she had prepared for me in a little room on the first floor of the house.

Next morning, waking up in a strange room in a strange house, the reality of the separation hit me with full force . . .

Then there were those who were favoured by the luck of the draw. One girl remembers her first impression of her foster father: 'He had Sephardi* eyes, like my mother. I felt at home at once . . .' And Helga Samuel was given every support and care by her foster parents. She describes the first meeting at Liverpool Street:

An extremely kind-looking couple stood there and a welcoming arm was placed around my shoulders . . . I was driven 'home' in a large car, complete with chauffeur – past St Paul's Cathedral, Buckingham Palace and other places of interest (although not to me that day, as

* A Jew from Spanish descent

my heart was filled with such uncertainty it is hard to describe and I had a lump in my throat), and I sat in the back of the car, still with that comforting arm around my shoulders . . .

On arrival at my new 'home', the maid opened the door, I saw a lovely open fire burning in the grate – the first thing – a cup of tea and something to eat and more kind words to help me to bear it all. I remember crying all that first day – the strangeness of it all – the sadness of having first to part with my mother – then with my sister – now being all on my own – in a strange country – a strange house – strange people – but with wonderfully kind faces.

So the days passed, difficult at first, mostly sign language, as I had only learned a few English words by this time . . . gradually getting used to my new environment. I had acquired a new 'sister' and 'brother' – everyone was doing their utmost to make me feel happy . . . children adapt and learn quickly and learn to forget even more quickly the sad things . . .

A lack of basic English could lead to weird experiences. One boy thought that 'To let' signs indicated a toilet. Another, on his first bus journey, noted down the name of a shop as a landmark for the return trip. It took a little time for him to realize that 'Bovril' was not a local retailer.

Herta Stanton stayed two days in London before travelling to her new home:

It was in Crawley. I had an address and in England you write the road first and the town last, whereas on the continent you did the opposite – the town first, then the street. It had the name of a house called Kingscourt and I asked for a ticket to Kingscourt and they gave me one. I arrived at a little halt in the country, some-where near East Grinstead. And there was nothing there. One man was stationmaster, porter, the lot. I showed him the address and he laughed. He realized what had happened. I remember there was a woman there who gave me a lovely red apple to eat because I was in such distress. They put me on a bus and the bus driver was told where to put me off. And that was my first impression of England.

After arriving at Liverpool Street and spending the night in London, Angela Carpos was sent off to Edinburgh with another girl.

Nobody told us it would take all night to get there. We sat up, waiting for the station called Edinburgh . . . We were told a lady would pick us up. When we arrived, in a right state, not having slept a wink and having nothing to eat, the platform emptied and there was no lady. A young man came and picked up our cases. We were very suspicious children and we started to scream. Nobody came to help. He jabbered in English and, before we knew where we were, we were in a car.

My friend said: 'I've got a penknife – you scream *Hilfe!* (Help! – which would have done a lot of good in Edinburgh) and I will stick the knife in his back.'

Letters from home contained frequent reminders to show appreciation. But gratitude came more easily with hindsight. Miss Harder was a spinster in her early fifties, who ran a small tobacconist's shop. She had continuously offered her services to the RCM committee as a foster parent, but they had never found a suitable child and perhaps also felt that she was too poor to cope. But when she heard about Lore Selo and her two sisters, whose mother did not want them to be parted, Miss Harder promptly offered to take all three and the committee was glad

Jewish refugee children on a train, shortly after crossing the German border

German refugee children embark in Holland for the journey to England.

12 December 1938: Children from Vienna arrive at Harwich. A special train takes them to Pakefield Holiday Camp in Lowestoft.

The children arrive at Customs in England.

Two of the youngest refugees: the boy is five years old and the girl is six.

A teenager arrives in England, tired and distressed.

little girl from a party of children from Berlin and Hamburg clutches
er doll. She is taken to a holiday camp at Dovercourt, near Harwich.

Refugee children wave from their chalets at Dovercourt holiday camp.

All the photographs in the inset are copyright © Wiener Library.

to accept. She even refused the offer of financial assistance, in case it led to another child losing his chance of coming to Britain.

Lore will never forget her first meeting with Miss Harder:

A lady dressed rather shabbily in old-fashioned clothes came towards us and into my hands she put a card on which the words 'Mother Love' were written. I knew a little English, just enough to understand what she meant to convey, but at the time my sisters and I were rather bewildered and, quite frankly, disappointed. We were young and frightened and I suppose we really had no idea what to expect, but we certainly never thought that our new foster mother would look so unattractive. We had even more of a shock when we saw her dingy home. It was a two-room flat in an old mansion block. She had given up her bedroom to the three of us and she slept in the sitting room on the sofa. It all seemed very cramped and poor and the flat was dark.

Those early weeks when we were miserable – we missed our mother and often cried – must have been very difficult for Miss Harder. She had to spend a good deal of her time in the shop and rush back to cook meals and care for us. Three tearful children who spoke very little of her own language cannot have been easy to love. But she was patient and understanding and even treated us to a holiday on the Isle of Wight, which, we found later, she could barely afford. She was helped to pay for it by friends and customers.

After a few months the three girls began to settle down. When a message came from a friend in Prague that their mother had disappeared, Miss Harder did everything she could to console them and they became very close. With the outbreak of war, the shop fell on harder times. When Miss Harder had to do without her assistant, Lore helped out:

We were too young to realize that it must have been a most worrying time for Miss Harder. Sometimes we were naughty, as children inevitably are.

Six months after the sisters arrived in England, Miss Harder died of consumption. The sisters were separated, Lore working as a maid and the others going to foster parents. Twenty years later, in a talk which was later broadcast on BBC Radio, Lore looked back:

> I think it is only now, after all these years, that I quite understand what a truly kind, wonderful and courageous woman Miss Harder was. She was my second mother for those few months. My sisters and I owe our lives to her but we can never repay her for her kindness, for having taken three unknown children into her home, given them love and understanding and compassion.

Ya'acov Friedler experienced two very different, but both very English, foster homes, adapting to both ways of life. Staying first of all with the Maggs, in a small country town, he learned the middle-class way of doing things:

> Mealtimes were the real lessons for me. Mrs Maggs instructed me how a young Englishman should use his knife and fork, drink his soup without making a noise, and never leave the table without permission from the head of the family. The slices of bread for tea were cut razor-thin, a habit that has stayed with me.
>
> One day, when I refused the slice of dried fruit cake

because I had already eaten all I could, Mr Maggs pointed out to me that a well-mannered young man leaves enough room for the cake because it is an integral part of tea. It might have been frivolous to worry about tea and cakes while the war for the very survival of Britain was raging, but I felt that these apparent trivialities were at the heart of what we were fighting for.

Happy though he was, Ya'acov wanted very much to be together with Solly, his brother, and the Maggs were not able to accommodate the two of them. They found a new billet in a working-class household. The Crooks, middle-aged and childless, made them welcome. There was just one problem:

They treated us with much love in the year we spent with them and it pains me still that we were forced to live a lie with them.

When it was first suggested that they take in two Jewish refugee boys from the continent, they made it plain that they would not have any German boys under their roof. It was impossible to explain to them the difference between German Nazis who were trying to destroy Britain and Jewish refugees from Germany.

We had to pretend we were Du[...]

pretence to the end.

The Crooks' old cottage had neith[...]
a bathroom. The parlour and kitchen [...]
The radio worked on a liquid acid batte[...]
be recharged every few months. Upstairs [...] [...]re
two bedrooms with no lights at all, and when we went
up to bed we would take a candle in a china holder and
snuff it out the moment we were between the sheets.

Margaret Olmer found her working-class foster
parents in the Midlands very anxious to learn as
much as possible about her background:

He worked in the local shoe factory and she worked in
a clothing factory. They had no children and lived in a
terraced house. She fretted when I went to grammar
school – because I was getting opportunities that she
never had . . . but they were quite cultured. She had
wanted to be a teacher. They weren't Jewish, but let me
go to Jewish classes.

The family who took in Lorraine Allard had a long-
term relationship in mind:

only son had a girlfriend who was not Jewish. By bringing me into the house, they hoped he would switch his affections. That I was only fourteen never entered their minds. In fact, their son did marry his girl-friend who converted*. They had an extremely happy marriage with four children.

In any case, Lorraine was far too preoccupied to think about romance. As the prospects of war increased, many children became obsessed with getting their parents out of Germany. For Lorraine it was her one and only thought:

I could not get across to my foster parents how bad things were in Germany. I set out in Lincoln knocking on people's doors. I found expensive areas and knocked on the doors of big houses and asked if they needed a cook or a gardener because that was the only way you could get people over without money being involved. Most of the time I knocked on doors and burst into tears; some-times, although I barely spoke any English, I could get some words out. I spent every spare moment doing this

* became Jewish

and I think if the war had waited a little I would have found someone to help. I did find homes for three other children, but it was hard to get my elderly parents out. My first boyfriend in Germany came to Lincoln, but the two girl cousins I found homes for didn't make it. Nor, unfortunately, did my parents.

Michael Brown's sister stayed with a family where he was able to visit. She was seven years old and he was ten:

. . . they put us in the same bed and we would weep and weep, both of us. She was absolutely distraught and missed her mother desperately. Later on, unfortunately, the mother of the house where my sister stayed died . . . it was hard for my sister because the father was a miser, heartless, and couldn't deal with a youngster in the house.

Ruth Michaelis felt betrayed from the time her mother brought her over to England and left her with the Reverend Stead and his family.

The only clear memory I have that gives any sort of insight into my feelings about my parents has to do with the big doll's house at the rectory. I was allowed to play with it for a while and I remember getting all the little dolls out of the doll's house and putting them into the rubbish bin, and when somebody had put them all back I did it again. I can remember being smacked for it but I did it again. It was quite compulsive. I think my feelings about people were that they were rubbish. I can remember being astonished at myself for doing it, having been told not to.

She was constantly promised that there was not going to be a war and that she would soon go back to her family. A sixth sense told her otherwise.

The total darkness of night without any street lights made me feel unsure . . . was anything there? I remember an awful feeling of there being nothing and scratching myself to test out if I was still alive because I was uncertain of whether I still existed.

Unhappy with the Steads, where she was beaten with a leather strap for wetting the bed, Ruth found a happier relationship with another family, but she could not rid herself of the insecurity.

I mistrusted people because they ditched you sooner or later, and important things they said could not be relied upon.

Having relatives in England was not always the bonus it was made out to be. Uncles and aunts were likely to be out of touch with what was happening to their relatives in Europe, and sometimes there were tensions and disagreements which had long been bubbling away beneath the surface.

Elli Adler remembers the reception her aunt gave her:

My aunt unpacked my suitcase and said what a lot of rubbish I had brought because I had brought books. My mother had packed classical books and also some of my own books, one in particular I was very fond of – a book about Greek mythology – and she deprived me of these books. She just took them away except for the *Jungle* books. I didn't get on with her very well. She said my mother should have packed more clothes, but I think my mother had packed all the clothes I had. I don't think my aunt realized just how hard up we were.

Not exactly overjoyed at the prospect of looking after her niece, Liesl Silverstone's aunt secretly attempted to shift the responsibility without her niece knowing:

I remember being shocked when I found my aunt's letter trying to farm me out at four pounds a week to an elderly couple. But I knew that she didn't want me. I also knew that my aunt was the one sister who couldn't cope in her family and who was constantly over-protected and smothered. She found it very difficult here as a refugee. I suppose I was all she needed.

In fact, I was the mother in that household, which was quite a burden. I was trying to hold it all together. I wasn't just seeing to my schoolwork, I was looking after her.

Some of the happiest memories are of small hostels that provided more of a family atmosphere than the foster homes. This was particularly so with hostels set up by individuals or by groups of sympathizers, rather than by religious or other charitable organizations. There was the contact with friendly adults, but not so close as to suggest to the children that their real parents no longer counted — a common resentment in foster homes. At the same time, the children could draw emotional strength from a shared experience.

Among those who set themselves the task of creating a hostel for orthodox children was Sybil Wulwick. Married in the summer of 1938 to the Reverend Geza Wulwick, who had been brought up in Czechoslovakia and who spoke fluent German, she and her husband settled in Middlesbrough and almost immediately started collecting money for refugee children. Their breakthrough was the free loan of a large Victorian house. Reverend Wulwick dedicated himself to the children's needs:

Because the hostel wasn't ready by the time the first batch of children arrived, we had to take them into our homes. My husband brought me two of the not-so-pretty girls who had felt left out. I suddenly had twins — two Hannahs. Our hearts went out to these children. One of them, Hannah Freulich (she was a plump little thing), had a letter inside her attaché case with a big box of talcum powder from her mother. The letter said:

'Please look after my little girl. I thank you from the bottom of my heart. Bath her every night and use this powder; she is used to it.' So I did.

The Schlesingers already had five of their own children including John, who was destined to become a leading film director. Bernard Schlesinger was a senior physician at Great Ormond Street Hospital for Sick Children; his wife, Winifred, a gifted musician and linguist. With their sympathetic, open-minded attitudes to young people, they came closest to the RCM ideal for a foster family. They bought a large house in Highgate with money left by a relative and set it up as a hostel. A matron was installed, and three helpers, one of whom did the cooking. There was room for twelve children. One of them remembers:

Mrs Schlesinger was at Liverpool Street to meet us all and we were very impressed that she spoke very fluent German. We were taken straight to Highgate. We were well received, well looked after, wanted for nothing; we were extremely lucky. There were five boys and seven girls in the group; we got on very well. We were enrolled in the local school, where we shared a class-room with the top form, who were probably thirteen or so. We must have seemed a lot of oddballs – probably dressed a bit funny, and so on. We had more or less individual teaching, but I don't quite know how they managed to teach the English children at the same time in the same room. It couldn't have been easy.

The extended family of the Schlesingers kept in touch over the years. Other foster children with happy memories did the same.

Chapter Five

Evacuated!

By early 1939, many felt that war with Germany was inevitable. There seemed to be no other way of stopping Hitler from taking over any part of Europe that he fancied. After marching into Austria in February 1938, he threatened to invade neighbouring Czechoslovakia on behalf of a German-speaking minority who lived there and wanted to be part of Germany.

The British government began preparing for war. In addition to building up the military, measures were put in hand for protecting the civilian population. An opinion shared by all the experts was that a declaration of war would be quickly followed by a massive air attack on London and other big cities. One estimate was for one hundred thousand bombs to fall on the capital within two weeks of the start of hostilities. An enormous number of casualties was expected. To try to reduce the suffering, plans were made to clear the cities of the sick, the handicapped and of children aged under fifteen – all those most at risk from aerial bombardment.

In September 1939, when Germany invaded Poland, and Britain and France declared war, there came a full-scale evacuation. Among the million and a half young people sent off to the safety of the countryside were between two to three thousand refugee children from Nazi-occupied Europe. Having just settled into new homes, they were once more on the move, nervous and worried about their future.

At the start of the operation, children went every day to school equipped with gas masks in cardboard boxes and carrying a small case ready packed – no one knew which day they would actually be leaving and the destination was secret.

When the day finally came, each child was tagged with a number for identification. There were sandwiches for the train or bus journey. Some children had last-minute treats of ice cream and sweets which made them sick. Weeping foster parents said goodbye to the children in their care. It was almost a rerun of the experience in Germany and Austria.

At the reception centres it was a return to 'cattle market' selection. The children were paraded around while householders took their pick. Many families had children forced on them by billeting officers. Local authorities appointed volunteers to go from door to door to see who had room and who didn't; those on the receiving end had no choice in the matter.

No child could be expected to enjoy the experience, but for refugee children evacuation was more than usually painful. Even those who had arrived in early 1939 or before did not as yet have complete command of English, and this made communication difficult. In rural areas the heavy regional accents added to the problem. The worst sufferers were those children who were placed in remote places, where strangers were suspect. Magda Chadwick, born in 1928, experienced this thinly veiled hostility:

Being evacuated away from my guardians was the most terrible incident in my life. Having only a smattering of English, I went to the Lake District. We went to the village hall and you stood there and people came and chose you. If your face fitted. They let brothers and sisters stay together and I stood with two sisters who were very kind to me. They asked if we were a family and I said, 'No, but I would like to be with them.' So the two girls went to a couple of spinsters who said that the farm next door needed a girl. But they got me there to be a housemaid. They asked me to wash the kitchen floor. I said I had never done it and I wasn't going to start.

I lived in the farmhouse. The country wasn't my style. I am a town person. There were no mod cons. The two sisters had a croquet lawn at their place – it was luck of the draw. I had to deliver the milk. In the dark, carrying two milk cans, I walked right into the wall because there was no light and I didn't know where I was going.

Very little advice was given to householders who received refugees. The local RCM committees followed up the refugee children after evacuation, but householders in rural areas rarely knew anything of Jewish customs. Pupils of an orthodox Jewish secondary school were greeted on arrival at Shefford with a welcoming ham omelette. With their lack of English, they were unable to explain why they chose to go hungry rather than go against the strict Jewish dietary laws.

The happiest results came when families gave their evacuees time to settle in and made some attempt to understand their cultural differences. One such family took in two sisters:

We said please take us because nobody wants us. So they went to the kitchen and discussed us and their hearts melted and that's how they took us both. It was a wonderful thing to do because they had no idea about the Jewish problem and all their family were wondering about them taking Germans. But that didn't last very long. While we were there we spent a very happy Christmas with her parents on a farm in Hertford and after the war, when my relatives came over from Holland on a visit, they met my uncle.

Kurt Weinburg's evacuation began disastrously but, thanks to his headmaster, it turned out better than he expected:

. . . I just assembled with all the other children at the school and we walked to the station and then went to Burgess Hill. We were billeted with various families and I remember the first family I was sent to didn't want to take me because I came from Germany. So whoever was in charge of billeting took me next door to the home of Mr Crombie. He was my headmaster, who was about to open the school in Cornwall. As I had no family and certainly no money, he took me with the school servant, two dogs and one other boy in his old Morris from Burgess Hill to London, and then we drove early in the morning from London all the way to Cornwall. I became a boarder and Mr Crombie gave me free schooling until I did matriculation* in 1942.

It was wonderful in Cornwall. For me it was freedom

* Examinations taken before entering university or college

– I was back in the countryside I loved. The school was small – only about thirty-five children. In London there was discipline with uniforms; down there there was no discipline and we didn't have to wear uniforms. I adopted one of Mr Crombie's dogs, a black cairn terrier – he more or less became my dog.

I joined the Boy Scouts troop and soon became patrol leader, and that gave me a lot of responsibility for the first time. I took my patrol camping and I organized the salvage collections of waste paper, tins and boxes.

In spite of evacuation to an apparently safe area, Peter Morgan has vivid memories of a more frightening side of wartime activity:

In 1939, we were evacuated to the Isle of Wight. I can't think of a worse place to have sent children. Whatever the Germans had left after bombing London, we got the lot. We were actually machine-gunned one Saturday afternoon, walking along the front at Ventnor. The plane just came in and shot at us as if the pilot had nothing better to do.

Peter went next to the Latymer School, which had been evacuated from Hammersmith to High Wycombe.

... standing at the top of the church at West Wycombe, on a clear night you could see St Paul's and you could see London burning.

He was still in the way of stray bombs. One landed in the middle of the school playing fields.

For most children, education half a century ago was pretty basic. All children were entitled to free education up to the age of fourteen. Thereafter, a limited number of free places at senior schools and universities was open to those judged to be the brightest. The rest were expected to leave school and go out to work to earn a living or take up technical training. As newcomers to the British education system, not to mention the English language, refugee children started with two obvious disadvantages. But in any case, however gifted, they were not encouraged to better themselves. The general view was that refugees belonged to the lower orders. When asked what he wanted to be, one young hopeful said that he wanted to be a doctor. The woman who was filling in the job-seeker's form said: 'I can't put that down – you must remember you are a refugee.'

When she came to England, aged five, Hannah was described as a bright, if naughty, child. The pattern continued throughout her time at school, leading her foster father to conclude that her education was a waste of time. What he did not know, until an RCM visitor winkled it out, was that Hannah wanted to study art. After some discussion he agreed that, provided Farnham Art School found Hannah's work sufficiently good to admit her, he would drop his objection to the idea. Hannah was duly offered and accepted a place at Farnham.

With evacuation and the RCM's preference for rural settings for foster homes and hostels, younger children were often isolated in small village primary schools, where they were a curiosity to the other children and to the staff. Struggling with an unfamiliar language, the simplest conversations were misinterpreted, as when Herbert Holzinger failed to understand why 'yes' was pronounced 'yessah' at school until someone explained that it was the respectful way to address the teacher: 'Yes, sir.'

> It was sometimes hard to separate being German from being Nazi. I didn't want to be known as a foreigner and I especially resented being called a German. 'Austrian' was not too bad, for, after all, Austria herself had been a victim of Nazism. I was furious when I was nicknamed 'Girder' at school, and wished I hadn't such a silly name as Gerda and a surname which I always had to spell out to people.

Vera Coppard, attending St Christopher's School at Letchworth, found it hard to take the persistent jokes about her being a German spy. The childish japes of putting a stink bomb in her locker caused her great anguish. Did they really hate her so much?

Another layer of guilt was added to the load of brighter children, who started pulling ahead of their classmates. Said one: 'I lied about my birth, but I realized I was different, and always coming top of the class did not help.'

Teachers too could be prejudiced. Even those who prided themselves on liberal views found it hard not to score points.

I remember an incident when we all went into a room which was rather cold and I shivered. The teacher with us said in her wonderfully piercing upper-class voice: 'People in England don't shiver when they come into a cold room. There isn't enough coal because *we're* fighting the *Germans.*'

Probably the greatest difficulty for the RCM was in satisfying the educational needs of the older children, who had already achieved a sound basic education. By rights, these young people should have been destined for college or university. Refugees, however, were refused state scholarships. Without funds to cover fees and lodging, most were cut off from higher education. Those who wanted to continue their studies usually had to attend evening classes or sign on for correspondence courses.

Among those who campaigned tirelessly for gifted youngsters was Greta Burkill. Greta, though born in Germany, went to school and university in Britain and married a Cambridge professor, Charles Burkill. As chairman of the Cambridge Refugee Committee – in effect, covering the whole of East Anglia – some eight hundred youngsters came within her province, although at the height of the evacuation this figure increased to two thousand.

With two daughters of her own, Greta expanded her family by taking in the son of a German socialist who had been sent to a concentration camp, and a Viennese boy who adopted her name by deed poll. She helped a succession of youngsters to take part-time degrees by getting them jobs as kitchen porters or trainee cooks. In one year alone she was overseeing twelve undergraduates, of whom eleven gained first-class degrees.

Eighty-one refugee children went to Bunce Court, Anna Essinger's school in Kent. It was a progressive school. Staff and pupils were on first-name terms. Anna Essinger, who had been dubbed *Tante Anna* in German, was known simply as TA. The emphasis was on self-reliance, with the children contributing to the upkeep of their school by making furniture and cleaning and repairing the building. But, unlike other progressive schools, classroom teaching was firmly rooted in the German tradition, with the highest priority given to academic excellence.

Clever, imaginative children like Leslie Brent did well at Bunce Court.

At first I shared a bedroom with five or six boys in the main part of the school building on the top floor. The school had very beautiful grounds, a lovely garden and a small wood; a large playing field; an open-air amphitheatre, which had been built by the children themselves in earlier years, in which plays were performed . . . The children did a lot of the work that needed to be done and it was an important part of the philosophy of Anna Essinger that children should be involved on a practical basis . . . My duties tended to gravitate from doing kitchen work to working in the workshop and in the garden. In the afternoon we played hockey and football. In the mornings we started off with gymnastics before breakfast, which some children found hateful, and once a week we organized a relay race. I enjoyed the physical side very much indeed.

I was one of many children who were very happy at

Bunce Court. To me it was a safe haven where I was treated with affection and respect; where I was taught well and made friends . . . It provided me with a very secure environment and a very good springboard for life, despite a total lack of teaching in the physical sciences. Although I was only there from early 1939 to the end of 1942, the influence it has had on me was out of all proportion to the time I spent there.

From the earliest days in England, Bunce Court was open to children whose families were victims of Nazi persecution. At least a dozen pupils were educated free of charge, with the promise that fees would be paid when the parents' situation improved.

Private benefactors enabled the school to build two new dormitories, while thirty of the youngest children were accommodated in an old farmhouse. There was never enough money for essentials. Hardly a week passed without Anna Essinger setting off for London on a fund-raising mission, invariably returning with promises to sponsor more refugee children. In May 1940, her problems were made worse by an evacuation order which transferred Bunce Court from Kent to Shropshire. The school occupied Trench Hall, a stately home which, having stood vacant for seven years, showed all the obvious signs of neglect. This was when Anna Essinger's philosophy of self-help came into its own, not least in transforming the jungle of a garden to provide food for the entire school.

How Bunce Court got through the war it is hard to imagine, but it did, and with flying colours, if the testimony of former pupils is anything to go by. It became a family within an institution, and there was greater contentment there than within the average hostel or foster home and most certainly a greater sense of personal fulfilment.

Chapter Six

After the War

In five years of war, many of those children who came over with the *Kindertransporte* grew up into young adults in Britain. They had put down roots, settling into jobs or even marrying and starting their own families. But times were hard for everyone. After the war, living conditions were often cramped and poor. There were few clothes and household goods to buy, and food was rationed. Interesting, well-paid jobs were hard to come by. Most of the young refugees found themselves in menial factory or office jobs, or in domestic work. There is a pile of file cases of talented young men and women longing for a more fulfilling life. As one of the few who had a highly successful career, Leslie Brent is the first to say that luck has played a big part in his life. His first break was to be spotted at Dovercourt as a star pupil. After the army, he studied zoology at Birmingham, which prepared him for his second stroke of good fortune. He was to be accepted as a postgraduate student at University College under Peter Medawar, one of the world authorities on immunology. He stayed on to be part of a research team, whose work on the mysteries of the immune system led to Medawar being awarded a Nobel Prize. In 1965, Leslie Brent was appointed Professor of Zoology at Southampton.

Alf Dubs (now Lord Dubs), who was one of the child refugees from Czechoslovakia, became a Labour MP and Director of the British Refugee Council. His success came through an early dedication to politics:

At grammar school in Manchester, other people of my age weren't interested in politics. But I was passionately involved in the 1945 election. My mum took me to

St Anne's-on-Sea for a week in a boarding house. The first election results came through at midday. There was a loudspeaker in the main square and people at the hotel sent me off to get the score. Since I was Labour I was delighted to be able to announce that we had one hundred and twenty seats against only thirty for the Conservatives. I remember someone groaning, 'Oh, my God, it's the end of England.'

Alf Dubs went to the London School of Economics and was elected to parliament in 1979.

A few refugees were able to draw on skills that they had acquired before they were uprooted. For example, Käthe Fischel, now a successful artist, was already an art student when she was forced to leave Czechoslovakia. Others, like Clive Milton, had to start from scratch. From working on a farm he went on to set up the Sheraton Patisserie chain.

Freddy Durst worked his way up to become a top jeweller. With his friend John Najmann, he learned his trade at evening classes.

We worked for three years for up to sixteen hours a day, saving what we could. Our aim was to put together a hundred pounds so that we would have enough to start on our own. After the war, we set up our own little workshop. When John went off to Germany to find his mother, who had survived Auschwitz, I was on my own for a while. That was when I bought my first bits and pieces of gold. I filed them up and made a few rings to sell to the Oxford Street shops. The problem was I didn't realize that after you sell something it takes a month to get payment. I should have opened a bank account, but at twenty-one that wasn't easy. But I got more and more orders and I was soon earning eight pounds a week.

It was the start of a career which led to the creation of the biggest jewellery manufacturing business in Britain.

In the early days after the war, feelings about Germany centred on hopes of finding relatives who had survived. The RCM had a flood of enquiries from children who were desperate to know what had happened to their parents. Tragically, only a few had survived the concentration camps. For those who did come through the war, reunions with their children were not always happy occasions.

The children had been encouraged to look to their own futures, not dwell on the past. Their experiences could not have been more of a contrast to those of their parents and when they came together they met as strangers. Often they did not even speak the same language. And this was only the beginning of the emotional pressures. It came as a terrible shock to realize that fondly remembered parents, who had once offered confidence and stability, were now themselves fragile and nervous. Few youngsters were able to cope, as Liesl Silverstone discovered:

Eventually I heard that my mother had survived. They found her in the mortuary at Mauthausen Camp. She must have made a little sound when the camp was liberated – so back she came from the dead. She was extremely ill with typhus.

When she was well enough she came here. We met again. I saw her last when I was twelve and now I was eighteen. There was an enormous gap. One of the first things she said to me was that I was the one left to her to make life all right again. I couldn't do it. It was no longer a mother-and-daughter relationship. How do you proceed with a mother who has been to Auschwitz? In retrospect, I realize that after the war I got a different mother back.

It was all too confusing and awful. The things we needed to say we were not ready to say to each other. She died before it could happen. She never cried after the war. She just carried on coping, like I did. So we were both denying things. We survived as best we could.

Liesl and her mother returned to Czechoslovakia, where Liesl was the only person of her own age-group left alive out of a Jewish community of sixty thousand in her home town. In 1948, she came back to England.

Ruth Michaelis was with her third foster family when her mother came to fetch her:

I had really settled down after being kicked out of my own country and then shunted from foster parent to foster parent. I didn't want to be uprooted again and my foster family wanted to keep me, so there was a battle royal between my foster mother and my mother.

After I was taken back to Germany, I was a very bolshie teenager. I refused to do anything. I refused to learn German. (I had forgotten it all and I flatly refused to learn.) I stayed six months before they gave in and let me come back to England.

My parents saw me off at Mainz. It was a difficult departure because I was trying to avoid saying goodbye to my parents. At that time I could not deal with my mother's wish to hug and kiss me. I kept my mother at arm's length, which must have been torture for her.

Ruth returned to her foster parents and to school in England.

The typical reaction of those who lost their family links with their first home was to try to block out the memories. One way was to go all out for a new identity, to become more British than the British. As one young man was heard to say about his nationality: 'I am as British as you are. In fact, I am more so because I chose it. I am double British.'

But however hard they tried, the shadow of earlier times remained – and remains to this day.

Sometimes it shows in little things, like Claire Barrington's dread of journeys:

> I have felt this anxiety all through my life; I never pre-
> pare for holidays. I don't like holidays; I don't like suit-
> cases or railway stations or booking tickets. I am always
> frightened of missing trains. I am always hours early
> when I am going somewhere . . .

Or Angela Carpos's dislike of card games:

> When I was staying with my grandmother in Germany,
> there was a very old Jewish man of eighty-two who
> taught me to play cards. He was dragged away one day.
> I still can't play cards today. My friends can't understand
> why I won't join in a game.

And there are those, like Harry Katz, who have shut themselves off from a world that can no longer be trusted.

> After the war, I tried through the Red Cross to trace my
> parents and sister. Maybe through a miracle they might
> be alive somewhere. But of course, being in the Warsaw

ghetto, none of them were. There was just my brother and myself. When he went to Palestine I hardly had any contact with him. I was practically alone for most of my life. I have difficulty making contact with people – perhaps because of my childhood – and it has kept on to the present day. I keep myself to myself, partly because I have trouble talking – a speech impediment – and it has kept me away.

Over the years, feelings about Germany have softened. Returning to Berlin, Peter Prager found himself thinking of his own experiences in a wider context.

I didn't feel any hatred . . . as a young boy I often felt it was a pity I was a Jew and that I couldn't be like the others. Perhaps if I had not been a Jew I would have done exactly like the others – I would have been like my classmates. Those who hate the Germans have to consider what they would have done in their place. It doesn't excuse the Germans, but it does mean that you have to examine how the Nazis came to power.

The past caught up with Leslie Brent when he was invited to lecture to the Polish Academy of Science. On a drive from Krakow, he came within twelve miles of Auschwitz.

It was the camp in which my family died. I didn't want to go there but as we got nearer I felt a strange compulsion to go . . .

In Auschwitz there is enough left to give one a pretty realistic idea of what it must have been like – the perimeter fence is there with the watchtowers and the gate, over which is written, incredibly, *Arbeit macht frei* (Work makes you free). None of the huts are left, but the brick foundations and the chimney stacks of each hut remain. So there are rows and rows of chimney stacks. I left some flowers. It was the first time I had wept uncontrollably in mourning for my family.

Leslie Brent has come to terms with his past, in so far as that is possible. Accompanied by his wife and son he has recently visited the town of his birth, now in Poland.

There are moments when I think about all this and I become overwhelmed with sorrow. But time has made it easier. I can now look back with a little more serenity.

Others, not so fortunate, are still puzzling on the nature of their true selves.

I came over at the age of three and a half. I still don't know where I belong. I was brought up in the Midlands. I went to a Christian school. I was no longer considered German, I was not considered English. I certainly wasn't Jewish – my Jewish background was not nurtured. I am neither German nor English. I am neither Gentile nor Jew. I would like to know, what is my identity?

The Refugee Children's Movement closed its files in December 1948. But, even today, over fifty years on, there is still a long way to go before the final chapter is written.

Chapter Seven

The Legacy of the
Kindertransporte

The story of the *Kindertransporte* is just one small part of the tragedy that engulfed Europe and the wider world between 1939 and 1945. Millions of families were forced from their homes to go in search of a place – any place – to live, often far away from where they were born and brought up. The ten thousand children who came to Britain from Germany, Austria and Czechoslovakia were lucky in that they survived, but losing their families and, in most cases, never seeing them again, left a terrible scar on their personalities, which could never heal entirely.

Have we learned from the experience? Only up to a point. The refugee problem is still with us. We are all familiar with the newspaper stories of asylum seekers who are trying to escape from persecution in their own countries or who are simply in pursuit of a better life. Throughout the world there are more refugees than ever before. According to the United Nations High Commissioner for Refugees there are a staggering fifty million displaced people and, of this number, around half are children. Most have had to flee their homes because of war, many are separated from their parents and are not being cared for by a responsible adult.

When we see figures like this, one reaction is to shut our minds thinking, perhaps, that there is nothing we can do about it, so why worry? But like all human crises that seem at first to be too big to handle, the important thing is to make a start. All else follows. That is one of the lessons of the *Kindertransporte*. As an act of national generosity it achieved good out of all proportion to its cost. It was a pity that more children could not have been welcomed in but, nevertheless, as word spread about the *Kindertransporte* more people became aware of what was happening in Germany, and more generosity was shown to those who were suffering through no fault of their own.

In today's world, credit should go to the excellent work being done by UNICEF and other United Nations agencies. In 2001, some sixteen thousand refugees under the age of eighteen with no families of their own were found permanent homes in many European countries – including Germany, where our story began. In fact, Germany now has an extremely good record for taking in refugees. One of the greatest achievements of humanitarian organizations operating in the Great Lakes region of Africa is a tracing programme, which has reunited seven thousand children with their families who had been set adrift by war.

That these examples are just dents in a huge problem cannot be denied. But, like the *Kindertransporte* in their time, they represent the first steps in coming to terms with our responsibilities to the wider world. In supporting charities, we help to raise awareness of the crisis and to persuade governments that simply to close the borders to outsiders is not an acceptable option.

Travelling across Europe nearly two hundred years ago, the American writer Washington Irving, creator of Rip van Winkle, came to the conclusion that, 'Until nations are generous they never will be wise. All selfishness may gain small ends but lose great ones.' Irving was not thinking of refugees when he wrote those words but they could well be applied to the current refugee crisis. It's about time that we took notice.

3 8002 01070 4874